There are days to be
blue when we're not
together. The best part
is that we have eachother
no matter what!
    I love you♥

A GIFT FOR: Roo

FROM: Sue

ME WITHOUT YOU IS LIKE...

BY LISA SWERLING
& RALPH LAZAR

COPYRIGHT © 2011 BY LISA SWERLING AND RALPH LAZAR

THIS EDITION PUBLISHED IN 2017 BY HALLMARK GIFT BOOKS, A DIVISION OF HALLMARK CARDS, INC., KANSAS CITY, MO 64141 UNDER LICENSE FROM CHRONICLE BOOKS. VISIT US ON THE WEB AT HALLMARK.COM.

ALL RIGHTS RESERVED. NO PART OF THIS PUBLICATION MAY BE REPRODUCED, TRANSMITTED, OR STORED IN ANY FORM OR BY ANY MEANS WITHOUT THE PRIOR WRITTEN PERMISSION OF THE PUBLISHER.

ISBN: 978-1-63059-815-0
BOK1070

MADE IN CHINA
0917

ME
WITHOUT
YOU
IS LIKE...

FOOT
WITHOUT
SHOE

HAIR
WITHOUT
DO

COW
WITHOUT
MOO

DOVE
WITHOUT
COO

BIKER WITHOUT TATTOO

MORNING
WITHOUT
DEW

RESTAURANT WITHOUT MENU

ESKIMO
WITHOUT
IGLOO

TANGO WITHOUT TWO

PARTY
WITHOUT
YAHOO!

PEAK WITHOUT VIEW

MUCH
WITHOUT
ADO

HARRY
WITHOUT
YOU-KNOW-WHO

BORED
BORED
BORED

PADDLE
WITHOUT
CANOE

CHIMNEY WITHOUT FLUE

CAT
WITHOUT
MEW

DETECTIVE WITHOUT A CLUE

KANGA
WITHOUT
ROO

← me

DOCTOR WITHOUT WHO

WRECK WITHOUT RESCUE

ZOO WITHOUT GNU

RAINBOW WITHOUT HUE

TEA WITHOUT BREW

BELLS WITHOUT BLUE

COCK
WITHOUT
A-DOODLE-DO

POOL WITHOUT CUE

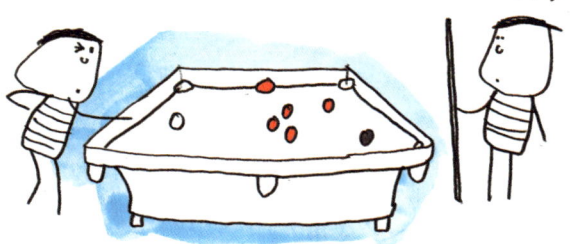

DOCTOR
WITH
FLU

A COOK
WITHOUT HIS
SOUS

A WITCH WITHOUT HER BREW

POLITICIAN WITHOUT ISSUE

SAINT WITHOUT VIRTUE

MERCENARY WITHOUT COUP

BALLERINA WITHOUT TUTU

KUBLAI KHAN WITHOUT XANADU

AN UNFINISHED HAIKU

RAM
WITHOUT
EWE

COOCHIE WITHOUT COO

YABBA WITHOUT DABBA-DOOOO!

MUSCLE WITHOUT SINEW

SNEEZE
WITHOUT A—

CHOO

DISCIPLE WITHOUT GURU

POTTY
WITHOUT
POO

COLD
FONDUE

PANDA WITHOUT BAMBOO

RUMBLE RUMBLE

A PICTURE THAT'S ASKEW

A FLAT
KAZOO

A NON-SPICY VINDALOO

A BOOK
THAT'S
OVERDUE

BOO

HOO

HOO

ME
WITHOUT
YOU!?

you being sneaky like always..?

WHAT WOULD I DO?

← me being clueless that you are sneakin'

PHEW!

This is the best

see you soon, my love ♥

IF YOU ENJOYED THIS BOOK
OR IT HAS TOUCHED YOUR LIFE IN SOME WAY,
WE'D LOVE TO HEAR FROM YOU.

PLEASE WRITE A REVIEW AT HALLMARK.COM,
E-MAIL US AT BOOKNOTES@HALLMARK.COM,
OR SEND YOUR COMMENTS TO:

HALLMARK BOOK FEEDBACK
P.O. BOX 419034
MAIL DROP 100
KANSAS CITY, MO 64141